Judith Rossell

INSPECTOR ROCKFORT
& the missing jewels

LARK BOOKS
A Division of Sterling Publishing Co., Inc.
New York

Inspector Rockfort and his young assistant, Nat, were having a holiday at the beach when the phone rang. It was Sergeant Baird of the local police.

"Inspector Rockfort," he said, "I am sorry to disturb your holiday, but we need your help. There has been a burglary at the Hotel Magnificent, and we are baffled. Can you help us?"

"We'll be right there," said the inspector. He turned to his assistant. "Come on, Nat, we've got a case to solve!"

"Now?" said Nat. "But it's nearly lunchtime…"

They met Sergeant Baird on the steps of the hotel. "This morning, while Countess Horne was having breakfast, a thief stole three precious jewels from her room," he explained. "I've interviewed the hotel staff, and they're all in the clear, so the thief must be one of the other guests."

"Have you searched their rooms?" Inspector Rockfort asked.

"Yes, Inspector, but I found nothing."

"Right," said Inspector Rockfort, "I'll need a list of the hotel guests. But first I'll go see the scene of the crime and talk to the Countess."

Room 1, Countess Horne

"Oh, Inspector!" cried Countess Horne. "My beautiful jewels were intact before breakfast, but look—while I was out three precious stones have been pried from this necklace and stolen. Please find them!"

Inspector Rockfort gave a polite bow. "I'm afraid the three jewels could be hidden anywhere; we must keep our eyes open. Luckily, there is something in this room that shows me exactly what they look like."

"Let's start looking straight after lunch," suggested Nat. "Did you notice the ten strawberries in here?"

Room 2, Mrs. Ponder

"Good morning, Mrs. Ponder," said Inspector Rockfort. "We are investigating a burglary and must speak to all the hotel's guests."

"How shocking," said Mrs. Ponder. "I'd be happy to help. And perhaps you could help me...I've tried all the jams and spreads here on the table, but I'd like to try a new flavor. Can you see a jar of anything different in the room?"

"Yes, Mrs. Ponder, there is one other flavor," said the inspector.

"As well as ten bananas," said Nat.

Room 3, Colonel Carp

"Fifty laps, every morning," said Colonel Carp. "You should swim, Inspector. Build up your muscles. But Mr. Tiler has a problem that needs brains, not muscles. He has to fix this broken mosaic—and we can't work out which three pieces he should use."

"That's just the kind of puzzle I'm good at," said Inspector Rockfort.

"And I can't work out why there are ten ice-cream cones in here," said Nat.

Room 4, Lady Coille

"Oh, Inspector," said Lady Coille, "I've been napping here since last Thursday, but I was constantly disturbed by the sound of water dripping. Can you find which tap to turn off?"

"Of course, Lady Coille," said Inspector Rockfort.

"I can see ten little cakes in here, Inspector," said Nat.

Room 5, The Tedd Family

"Oh, Inspector," said Mrs. Tedd, "my children are so fussy. I'm trying to buy them each an ice-cream cone, but it's impossible!

- Terry won't have anything pink or green.
- Trevor won't eat cherries.
- Tessa wants topping, but not chocolate topping.
- And Tina insists that everyone must have the same.

Please help me!"

"Don't worry, Mrs. Tedd," said the inspector. "There is one ice-cream cone that will please everyone."

"It would please me to eat the ten apples I can see," said Nat.

Room 6, Mr. and Mrs. Stipple

"We always sprint around the park right after breakfast, Inspector," said Mr. Stipple. "And then we have a rest and observe the wildlife. Today, we are looking for butterflies. Can you see any?"

"Yes," said Inspector Rockfort. "I can see ten."

"I can't see any butterflies," said Nat, "but I can see ten sandwiches."

Room 7, The Gibber Family

"Good morning, Mr. and Mrs. Gibber," said Inspector Rockfort. "I'd like to ask you—"

"Hi there, Inspector," interrupted Mrs. Gibber. "You're just the guy we need! The wind blew four of our tickets away. But we all want a ride! Can you spot the missing tickets for us? We need five consecutive tickets, including this one."

"No problem," said the inspector.

"And I can spot ten spoons," said Nat.

Room 8, Ms. Dune

"Ms. Dune," said Inspector Rockfort, "we are investigating a burglary."

"Oh really?" replied Ms. Dune. "Well I don't know anything about that; I came straight here this morning. I'm trying to find ten shells exactly the same as the one Mrs. Bill is holding."

"That shouldn't be too difficult," said the inspector.

"I don't see the ten shells," said Nat, "but I can see ten cherries."

Room 9, Mr. Wade

"Good morning, Inspector," said Mr. Wade. "Perhaps you can help me. I want to buy a bucket, a spade, and a ball. I don't mind what color they are, as long as they all match."

"Well," said Inspector Rockfort, "I can see one matching combination."

"And I can see ten pieces of cheese," said Nat.

Room 10, Miss Fringe

"Madam," called the inspector, "we are investigating a burglary."

"How interesting," said Miss Fringe. "I'd be happy to answer your questions. But I'm busy looking for the money I dropped. Can you see it from up there?"

"I can see five coins," said Inspector Rockfort.

"I can see ten sausages," Nat added.

Room 11, Mr. and Mrs. Bounder

"Good morning, Inspector," said Mr. Bounder. "You're just the person we need. I'm good at darts, but terrible at adding. To win one of those three big prizes at the top, I need to hit three numbers with three darts. I've already hit one, and I have two darts left. Which numbers do I need to hit in order to add up to one of the numbers on the prizes?"

"Hmm," said Inspector Rockfort, "there's only one big prize you can possibly win, and the numbers you need are...leave those fries alone, Nat."

"What about the ten sweets?" Nat asked.

Room 12, Mr. Streak

"Oh, Inspector," said Mr. Streak. "Please help me! I want to buy something sweet for my girlfriend, but she is very particular. She only likes fruit flavors, and no more than two flavors mixed together. And she hates hearts and flowers! What can I buy her?"

"It's tricky, but I can see three possibilities," said Inspector Rockfort.

"Speaking of sweet things, I can see ten donuts," Nat said.

"Another case solved," said Inspector Rockfort.

"Thank you so much, Inspector," Countess Horne said. "I thought I'd never see my lovely jewels again! What about the thief?"

"Ah, we know who the thief is," said the inspector.

"We do?" asked Nat.

"Yes," said Inspector Rockfort. "The thief was very careless and left many clues. Every time one of the jewels was hidden, the thief left something behind—and picked something up. Now do you know who it is?"

SEARCH · SEEK · SOLVE · SOLUTIONS

● The puzzle solved by Inspector Stilton
○ The hidden shapes spotted by Nat (there are actually 11, not 10!)

Room 1, Countess Horne

Room 2, Mrs. Ponder

Room 3, Colonel Carp

Room 4, Lady Coille

Room 5, The Tedd family

Room 6, Mr. and Mrs. Stipple